PRAYERSCRIPTS

PROSPERITY
T H R O U G H   T H E
BL🗲🗲D

60 DAYS OF PRAYERS FOR
UNLOCKING HEAVEN'S WEALTH &
WALKING IN COVENANT INCREASE

CYRIL OPOKU

Prosperity Through the Blood: 60 Days of Prayers for Unlocking Heaven's Wealth and Walking in Covenant Increase

Published by *Quest Publications*

ISBN: 978-1-988439-72-3

Cover design by *Quest Publications (questpublications@outlook.com)*

Unless otherwise indicated, all Scripture quotations are taken from the World English Bible WEB, which is in the public domain. For more information, visit: www.worldenglish.bible

This book is a work of devotional encouragement. It is not intended to replace biblical study, pastoral counsel, or professional therapy.

Printed in the United States of America.

First Edition: August 2025

For more books like this, visit *PrayerScripts:* https://prayerscripts.org

CONTENTS

PREFACE

"…though he was rich, yet for your sakes he became poor,
that you through his poverty might become rich."
— 2 Corinthians 8:9 WEB

I didn't always believe prosperity was my portion. For years, I lived with a survival mindset—grateful for salvation, yet unsure if abundance was truly part of the gospel. But as I searched the Scriptures and encountered the covenant more deeply, everything changed. I discovered that Jesus did not die for me to live in lack. He became poor, that I through His poverty might become rich—not just in spirit, but in every good thing.

This book, *Prosperity Through the Blood*, is born out of that revelation. It is the fifth installment in *The Blood Covenant Series*, following *Pardon Through the Blood, Protection Through the Blood, Prevail Through the Blood* and *Preservation Through the Blood*. Here, we focus specifically on unlocking the wealth of heaven—not as a get-rich-quick formula, but as a Spirit-led journey into kingdom abundance that glorifies God and blesses others.

These prayers are prophetic. They are not timid whispers; they are declarations of truth grounded in Scripture and sealed in Christ. As you pray them, expect things to shift—mindsets to change, doors to open, provision to come, and legacies to be restored. The blood has already made the way. Now it's time to walk in it.

Till He Comes,
Cyril O. *(Illinois, August 2025)*

INTRODUCTION

The blood of Jesus is not only for our salvation—it is the foundation of our inheritance. It speaks of redemption, healing, protection, and yes, prosperity. This book is a call to boldly believe in what the blood of Jesus has truly accomplished for us: not only freedom from sin, but access to divine abundance. Prosperity is not a worldly desire—it is a kingdom reality, purchased at the highest cost and backed by the covenant of the cross.

In a world consumed by fear of lack, economic uncertainty, and unstable systems, God's people must remember: we are not governed by the systems of man, but by the eternal promises sealed in Christ's blood. This is more than financial gain—it is provision for purpose, sufficiency for every assignment, and legacy for generations. You were redeemed not to barely survive, but to thrive—spiritually, emotionally, relationally, and materially.

This 60-day journey is designed to help you align your faith with the finished work of Christ. Each day, you will engage with Scripture, declare prophetic truth, and pray Spirit-led prayers that activate covenant prosperity in every area of your life. The blood speaks—and it speaks abundance. It's time to listen, believe, and walk in the overflow.

HOW TO USE THIS BOOK

This book is structured as a 60-day journey of prayer and prophetic declaration. Each day includes:

- A **topical focus** tied to covenant prosperity
- A **key Scripture**, quoted in the World English Bible
- A **Spirit-led prophetic prayer** rooted in that Scripture

Here's how to get the most out of it:

1. **Set aside daily time** to pray—ideally in the morning, when you can declare God's promises over your day.

2. **Read the Scripture out loud** to align your faith with the Word.

3. **Pray the prophetic prayer** slowly, with your heart engaged. Personalize it for your life, your family, and your circumstances.

4. **Keep a journal** to record what God is revealing, doing, and providing as you move through this journey.

5. **Repeat prayers** as needed. If a certain day's prayer deeply resonates with you, revisit it often. The Word never expires.

This book is not just for reading—it's for warring, declaring, and possessing what Jesus purchased. The blood has spoken. Now, echo it in prayer until prosperity becomes your reality.

DAY 1

CHRIST BECAME POOR FOR ME

"For you know the grace of our Lord Jesus Christ, that though he was rich, yet for your sakes he became poor, that you through his poverty might become rich."
— 2 Corinthians 8:9 WEB

Righteous Redeemer, I thank You for the lavish grace poured out through the blood of Your Son. I lift my voice in bold declaration: I refuse to live beneath the covenant that Christ has sealed with His blood. Jesus, though You were infinitely rich, You chose poverty—not for Yourself, but for me and my household. You took the full weight of lack, insufficiency, and deprivation so that I might step boldly into the abundance You secured.

By Your blood, I access every inheritance of prosperity—not just for survival but for divine flourishing. My hands are anointed to multiply. My work is blessed. I declare that financial barrenness is broken off me and my lineage. We will not toil under scarcity when the blood has spoken better things for us.

Lord, let the evidence of Your sacrifice manifest in my daily provision. Let there be a shift in my bank accounts, my business, my stewardship, and my legacy. I speak divine prosperity over my family. We receive what the cross purchased—nothing lacking, nothing broken.

In Jesus' name, Amen.

DAY 2

BLOOD-PURCHASED KINGSHIP

"They sang a new song, saying, 'You are worthy to take the book and to open its seals: for you were killed, and bought us for God with your blood out of every tribe, language, people, and nation, and made us kings and priests to our God; and we will reign on the earth.'"
— Revelation 5:9-10 WEB

Holy Lamb of God, You were slain, and with Your precious blood, You bought my family and me out of obscurity into royalty. I rise in prophetic understanding today: we are no longer bound, nameless, or without inheritance. We are blood-bought royalty. Dominion runs in our spiritual DNA.

Because You have made us kings and priests, we walk with authority. I decree that everything attempting to enslave us financially must bow to the voice of the blood. You didn't just save us for heaven—you crowned us to reign on earth. Every system, environment, and economic realm must now yield to the kingly anointing You placed on our lives.

Let our decisions be bathed in wisdom. Let our resources multiply supernaturally. Let our influence stretch wide, and our impact go deep. I call forth the manifestation of divine rulership in my family, in our finances, and in our fields of influence. We reign—not by pride, but by purchased right.

In Jesus' name, Amen.

DAY 3

HEIRS OF THE KINGDOM

"...and if children, then heirs—heirs of God and joint heirs
with Christ..."
— Romans 8:17 WEB

Abba Father, I step into the full understanding of my place in You.
I am not an outsider—I am a rightful heir. Through the blood of
Jesus, I've been adopted, accepted, and enthroned as a co-heir with
Christ. What belongs to Him is now mine—not by merit, but by
covenant.

I activate my inheritance today. I will not live as though I am
fatherless, landless, or abandoned. I lay claim to spiritual,
emotional, and financial wealth that flows from being joined to
Christ. The same favor that surrounds Him now surrounds me. The
same supply that sustains heaven now sustains my household.

Father, teach me to walk in my inheritance with boldness, with
humility, and with clarity. Let my family come into full awareness
of what we possess in You. Let generational lack be broken, and
generational wealth—righteous wealth—begin to rise. We walk as
joint heirs, knowing that no good thing will You withhold.

In Jesus' name, Amen.

DAY 4

CURSE OF LACK BROKEN

"Christ redeemed us from the curse of the law, having become a curse for us... that the blessing of Abraham might come on the Gentiles through Christ Jesus..."
— Galatians 3:13-14 WEB

O Blood Redeemer, I thank You that the curse has been shattered by the cross. You became the curse so I could carry the blessing. The generational strongholds of lack, limitation, and financial despair are demolished because of what You bore on that tree.

I claim the blessing of Abraham today—not in theory, but in full experience. I declare that my family is blessed going out and coming in. Our baskets overflow. Our barns are full. What once drained us now multiplies in our hands. The blood has reversed every word, pattern, and cycle of poverty.

Let the evidence of divine reversal show up in our finances, in our real estate, in our ideas, in our giving. I walk in covenant prosperity because You carried the weight of my insufficiency. I declare the curse is not just broken—it is forbidden from reattaching itself. The blessing rests on us.

In Jesus' name, Amen.

DAY 5

REDEEMED FROM POVERTY

"In him we have our redemption through his blood, the forgiveness of our trespasses, according to the riches of his grace."
— Ephesians 1:7 WEB

Mighty Redeemer, I thank You for the wealth of grace that flows from Your blood. This is not cheap grace—it is rich, weighty, and overflowing. Through that blood, I've been bought back from every form of bondage—including financial affliction and poverty.

Redemption means my debt is canceled. Redemption means my dry seasons have an expiration date. I decree that my household walks in redeemed economics—where heaven governs our increase. We are no longer under financial oppression. The blood has paid our ransom and secured our release.

Let the riches of Your grace be evident in every area of our lives. Let favor rest on our work, our hands, and our hearts. Let doors open not by manipulation but by the mystery of blood redemption. We are not broke; we are blood-bought and abundantly supplied.

In Jesus' name, Amen.

DAY 6

Eternal Inheritance Secured

"For this reason he is the mediator of a new covenant, since a death has occurred for the redemption... so that those who are called may receive the promise of the eternal inheritance."
— Hebrews 9:15 WEB

Everlasting Mediator, thank You for dying my death and securing my future. You gave everything so I could gain everything in Your name. Your blood did not just purchase momentary help—it sealed the promise of an eternal inheritance for me and my family.

I walk in this new covenant with confidence. I do not waver, doubt, or shrink back. My inheritance is sure. I decree lasting abundance in my life—not based on market trends but on covenant truth. I lay claim to the lands, the legacy, and the provision You designed for me.

Father, I align my thoughts, decisions, and actions with this eternal wealth. Let my family prosper not only materially but generationally. Let our wealth be rooted in righteousness. May our storehouses never run dry. Our portion is eternal, and our Provider is unchanging.

In Jesus' name, Amen.

DAY 7

QUALIFIED FOR PROVISION

"...giving thanks to the Father, who made us fit to be partakers of the inheritance of the saints in light; who delivered us out of the power of darkness, and translated us into the Kingdom of the Son... in whom we have our redemption, the forgiveness of our sins."
— Colossians 1:12-14 WEB

Faithful Father, I rise with gratitude today, knowing I am no longer disqualified by sin, shame, or scarcity. Your blood has qualified me. You made me fit—not man, not my works. You pulled me out of darkness and placed me into the light of divine provision.

I am a partaker of the inheritance of the saints. That means lack cannot lay hold of me. It means insufficiency cannot have dominion over me. You have already delivered my family from the grip of financial darkness. I walk in newness of provision today.

I speak over my household: we are qualified to receive, qualified to build, qualified to inherit, and qualified to multiply. The blood has spoken for us, and we align ourselves with its voice. Our portion is not crumbs—it is covenant-level provision.

In Jesus' name, Amen.

DAY 8

PEACE PURCHASED FOR PROVISION

"But he was pierced for our transgressions. He was crushed for our iniquities. The punishment that brought our peace was on him..."
— Isaiah 53:5 WEB

Prince of Peace, I thank You for bearing the full burden of punishment so that I could live in divine peace. Not just peace in my heart—but peace in my provision. Your blood bought rest from financial torment, from anxiety over bills, and from the dread of insufficiency.

I embrace the peace that flows from the cross. No more striving. No more toiling under the pressure of lack. The blood has settled it. I will eat in plenty and be satisfied. My family will know what it means to lie down in green pastures, for the Shepherd has already paid the price.

Let tranquility flood our finances. Let harmony reign in our financial decisions. I declare that divine order, supernatural ease, and holy abundance rest upon my household. We are no longer scattered—we are settled, prospering in the peace that was purchased in blood.

In Jesus' name, Amen.

DAY 9

JUSTIFIED TO PROSPER

"...being justified freely by his grace through the redemption that is in Christ Jesus, whom God set forth to be an atoning sacrifice through faith in his blood..."
— Romans 3:24-25 WEB

Holy Justifier, You declared me righteous, not by merit but by blood. I receive the full weight of that justification today. I am not condemned, unworthy, or disqualified. I am justified to prosper, justified to increase, justified to walk in divine supply.

By faith in Your blood, I access my portion. I don't earn it—I believe for it. Every accusation that would block my blessing is silenced by the blood. Every guilt-ridden memory that speaks of disqualification is overruled. I am justified to rise.

Let that justification speak in business deals, in financial decisions, and in family wealth. Let it echo through every closed door and open the way. My family will prosper—not in arrogance, but in the humility of grace received through blood.

In Jesus' name, Amen.

DAY 10

Kingly Abundance Released

"...to him who loves us, and washed us from our sins by his blood—and he made us to be a Kingdom, priests to his God and Father..."
— Revelation 1:5-6 WEB

Majestic King, You have not only cleansed me—you have crowned me. Through Your blood, You established me and my family as a kingdom. No longer beneath, no longer outsiders—we operate in the abundance of royalty.

Let kingly provision flow through our lives. I decree we live above the systems of this world. We are not beggars—we are kingdom builders. Let priestly stewardship and royal abundance mark every financial endeavor we take.

I walk in wealth not for selfish gain, but for kingdom advancement. My household is blessed to be a blessing. We carry the dignity of kings and the devotion of priests. Through Your blood, the throne room has become our inheritance.

In Jesus' name, Amen.

DAY 11

BOLDLY ACCESSING HEAVENLY RESOURCES

"Having therefore, brothers, boldness to enter into the
holy place by the blood of Jesus,"
— Hebrews 10:19 WEB

O God of all glory, I come today with boldness purchased by the priceless blood of Jesus! I do not approach You timidly or from a distance, but as one covered, cleansed, and consecrated by the blood of the Lamb. Through the torn veil, I step into the fullness of the heavenly storehouse, claiming every spiritual and material resource ordained for me and my family.

By this blood, I declare that I have unrestricted access to divine strategies, provision, wisdom, and answers. Every need I have is met not according to the world's economy, but by the riches of Your glory in Christ Jesus. Father, I refuse to live beneath what Jesus died to give me. Let the floodgates of provision be opened over my household. Let healing flow, let provision flow, let favor overflow, because I stand where only the blood can take me—before Your throne of grace and glory.

I boldly decree that no barrier, curse, or lack can deny me now. I access the treasury of heaven through this covenant of blood. My family and I walk in the overflow. We are blessed and not burdened, supplied and not struggling, in Jesus' mighty name.

In Jesus' name, Amen.

DAY 12

ACCESSING DIVINE FAVOR AND CONNECTION

"But now in Christ Jesus you who once were far off are made near in the blood of Christ."
— Ephesians 2:13 WEB

Righteous Redeemer, I thank You for bringing me near—not only to Yourself but also to divine opportunities, people, and places. By the blood of Jesus, the wall of separation is demolished, and I step into covenant favor. Where once I was distant from destiny helpers and divine doors, now I am brought near. My family and I are aligned with Your purposes and positioned for breakthrough relationships.

Father, because of the blood, every connection we need for our next level is drawn to us by divine magnetism. Let favor go before us like a shield. Bring the right voices, the right partnerships, the right opportunities at the right time. By the blood, we are no longer strangers or outsiders—we are heirs of divine access.

I decree open doors that no man can shut. I decree kingdom relationships that bless, elevate, and prosper. I declare that the blood draws mentors, investors, intercessors, and covenant allies into our orbit. We are no longer far—we are fully present in the flow of God's favor.

In Jesus' name, Amen.

DAY 13

PROSPERITY IS MY COVENANT PORTION

"Wealth and riches are in his house. His righteousness
endures forever."
— Psalm 112:3 WEB

Great Provider, I lift my voice in the authority of covenant. By the
blood of Jesus, I claim what is rightfully mine—prosperity with
purpose, increase with integrity, and wealth that brings You glory.
You have declared that wealth and riches are not the pursuit of the
wicked, but the inheritance of the righteous. I declare this over my
household: wealth belongs here, and riches are established under
the covering of Christ's righteousness.

By the blood, I release every financial breakthrough that has been
delayed or stolen. Let the blessing rest in my house—not just in my
hands, but in my legacy. I will use these resources to build, bless,
and advance Your Kingdom.

I uproot every mindset of lack, poverty, and limitation. I plant the
truth of Your Word in the soil of my faith: the righteous shall never
beg bread. Let prosperity arise and be established, for the blood has
signed my access. My family shall not live hand to mouth—we live
from glory to glory and from overflow to overflow.

In Jesus' name, Amen.

DAY 14

Standing on Better Promises

"But now he has obtained a more excellent ministry, by so
much as he is also the mediator of a better covenant, which
has been enacted on better promises."
— Hebrews 8:6 WEB

Almighty Covenant-Keeper, I honor the One who mediates for me
by His own blood. I stand today, not on the shaky ground of earthly
hope, but on the solid rock of a better covenant. This blood-sealed
covenant carries better promises—promises of prosperity, peace,
preservation, and purpose for me and my entire household.

I reject the inheritance of the old man and the curses of the past. I
embrace the better—better blessings, better access, better supply.
The blood of Jesus enforces every promise and guarantees its
delivery. I declare that my family walks under the blessing of
Abraham, the provision of Isaac, and the favor of Joseph, because
Christ is the fulfillment of all covenant promises.

Let every word You've spoken over us come to pass swiftly. Let our
lives be living proof that the new covenant is not only spiritual but
practical. Every promise You made, sealed with blood, we receive
with faith and thanksgiving. No devil can annul it, and no demon
can reverse it.

In Jesus' name, Amen.

DAY 15

No Lack in My Life

"Yahweh is my shepherd: I shall lack nothing."
— Psalm 23:1 WEB

Shepherd of my soul, I declare today under the blood of Jesus that lack has no place in my life. You lead me, feed me, and cover me. Because I am in covenant with You through the blood of the Lamb, I declare with boldness: I shall not lack—spiritually, emotionally, relationally, or financially.

You are my Source, not my job, not people, not circumstances. The blood has purchased my sufficiency. Every area of insufficiency bows to Your shepherding grace. Let overflow be my portion, and divine provision be my reality. My table is spread, even in the presence of opposition, because the covenant speaks for me.

My family is not forsaken. Our needs are supplied in abundance. I cancel the voice of scarcity and command every resource we need to locate us swiftly. The Shepherd who shed His blood for us is watching over every detail of our provision.

In Jesus' name, Amen.

DAY 16

GENERATIONAL BLESSING BY THE BLOOD

"I will establish my covenant between me and you and
your offspring after you throughout their generations for
an everlasting covenant, to be a God to you and to your
offspring after you."
— Genesis 17:7 WEB

Eternal God of covenant, I rise today to declare: the blood of Jesus
has grafted me into an everlasting lineage of blessing. What You
promised to Abraham, You fulfilled in Christ, and now that promise
rests on me and my seed. My family is marked for generational
prosperity and purpose, not by works but by blood.

I invoke the everlasting covenant over every child, every
grandchild, and all those who carry my name and legacy. I declare
that cycles of poverty, sickness, and failure are broken. We are not
cursed—we are covenant people! The blood of Jesus speaks into the
future, calling forth destiny, protection, provision, and honor for
my descendants.

Let every generational gate swing open for the purposes of God. I
speak prosperity that multiplies and righteousness that endures.
The blood has signed it, and heaven enforces it. This covenant is not
fragile—it is forever.

In Jesus' name, Amen.

DAY 17

LET THE BLOOD SPEAK INCREASE

"...to Jesus, the mediator of a new covenant, and to the
sprinkled blood that speaks better than that of Abel."
— Hebrews 12:24 WEB

O Jesus, Mediator of my prosperity, I thank You for the blood that
still speaks. It does not speak vengeance—it speaks increase, access,
and advancement. Every time the enemy accuses, the blood
intercedes. Every time lack tries to speak, the blood speaks louder.

Let the voice of Your blood silence every voice of limitation in my
life. Let it echo through the courts of heaven and the circumstances
of earth: I am redeemed, I am blessed, I am multiplied. The blood
declares increase over my home, my business, my finances, and my
future.

I align myself with what the blood is saying. I reject every report of
decrease, delay, or denial. My family is under the divine
proclamation of abundance. Better things are our portion—better
doors, better outcomes, better supply.

In Jesus' name, Amen.

DAY 18

POWER TO PRODUCE WEALTH

"But you shall remember Yahweh your God, for it is he
who gives you power to get wealth…"
— Deuteronomy 8:18 WEB

Yahweh my God, I remember You today as the One who gives power—not just promises. Your blood-bought covenant empowers me to create, multiply, and steward wealth. I do not wait for handouts; I activate divine capacity. Because of the blood, my hands are blessed, my ideas are inspired, and my labor is fruitful.

I declare that I and my family are wealth creators, kingdom financiers, and stewards of abundance. Let the anointing to innovate and increase rest mightily upon us. I cancel every generational curse of financial failure and unlock the ability to prosper in every season.

Father, let contracts be awarded, let clients be drawn, let streams multiply. Give me strength to build, wisdom to manage, and heart to give. I prosper by covenant, not by chance.

In Jesus' name, Amen.

DAY 19

ABUNDANT LIFE OVER MY FINANCES

"For the life of the flesh is in the blood..."
— Leviticus 17:11 WEB

Holy God, I release the life-flow of the blood of Jesus into every financial area of my life. I decree: no more dead ends, no more barren accounts, no more lifeless business endeavors. Where the blood flows, life reigns—and I declare abundant life in my finances and family resources.

Every dying dream, every withering investment, every paralyzed opportunity—I speak resurrection power by the blood. Let the same life that raised Christ flow into my economic reality. I curse stagnation and command the blessing of divine circulation.

Let financial life surge—unexpected income, supernatural debt cancellations, multiplied seed, and preserved harvests. The blood secures vitality and vigor, not just for my body but for my financial house.

In Jesus' name, Amen.

DAY 20

JUSTIFIED TO RECEIVE GOD'S BEST

"Much more then, being now justified by his blood, we will be saved from God's wrath through him."
— Romans 5:9 WEB

Merciful Justifier, I praise You for the verdict spoken over my life: not guilty! By the blood of Jesus, I am justified and qualified to receive every good and perfect gift. I do not stand in condemnation, and I do not live under guilt. I am an heir, not a beggar.

Every blessing You've stored up for me is now released without hindrance. The blood has silenced every accuser. Shame has no hold, and unworthiness is not my portion. I receive Your best—not by merit, but by mercy secured in blood.

Let abundance come swiftly. Let provision be unstopped. Let prosperity flow freely. I am justified to receive divine supply, favor, promotion, and overflow.

In Jesus' name, Amen.

DAY 21

HEIR, NOT A BEGGAR

"Therefore you are no longer a bondservant, but a son; and
if a son, then an heir of God through Christ."
— Galatians 4:7 WEB

Father, I thank You for the blood of Jesus that has changed my
identity forever. I am no longer a slave to lack, limitation, or the lies
of the enemy. I stand today not as a servant begging for scraps, but
as a rightful heir to the abundance of Your house. The blood has
purchased my sonship, and I boldly take my place as one who walks
in the full rights and benefits of covenant inheritance.

Lord, I renounce every mindset of poverty, every whisper of
unworthiness, and every generational curse of insufficiency. I am
not cursed—I am covered. I do not grovel—I govern. I am seated
with Christ in heavenly places, and all that the Father has is mine
through Him. I operate from the riches of grace, not the rags of self-
effort.

Let this blood-bought revelation saturate my family. May we walk
with the dignity of heirs, not with the fear of orphans. May doors
open to us, not by manipulation, but by divine inheritance. We
declare that favor is our portion, wealth is our responsibility, and
prosperity is our rightful station—because we are sons, not slaves.

In Jesus' name, Amen.

DAY 22

DRINKING FROM THE COVENANT CUP

"He took the cup after supper, saying, 'This cup is the new
covenant in my blood, which is poured out for you.'"
— Luke 22:20 WEB

O Covenant-Keeping God, I lift the cup of Your blood and drink
deeply of all You have provided. This is not a mere symbol—it is a
living agreement sealed in the blood of Jesus. I receive into myself
the riches of divine provision, favor, and fullness that this covenant
guarantees.

As I drink from this cup by faith, I ingest supernatural supply. Let
every lack in my life be filled with Your fullness. Let every dry well
spring up again. Let divine wisdom come, divine opportunities
arise, and divine connections manifest. I drink into wealth, not just
for myself, but for generations to come. This cup breaks the curse
of not enough and establishes the blessing of more than enough.

Let my household be saturated with covenant favor. Let every child
of mine be clothed in glory and supplied with heaven's best. We will
not live by the sweat of our brow, but by the Word of covenant
sealed in blood. As for me and my family, we drink of Your
abundance until our cup overflows.

In Jesus' name, Amen.

DAY 23

THE BLOOD ON OUR DOOR

"The blood shall be to you for a token on the houses where you are. When I see the blood, I will pass over you, and no plague will be on you to destroy you..."
— Exodus 12:13 WEB

Mighty Deliverer, I apply the blood of Jesus to the doors of my finances, my business, my household, and my legacy. Just as in Egypt, when the destroyer saw the blood and passed over, so today, every spirit of financial ruin, every unexpected loss, and every economic plague must pass over me.

By the authority of the blood, I declare that my family is immune from cycles of debt, sudden disasters, and generational poverty. Our lives are marked by divine exemption. Let insurance failures, market crashes, and business disruptions see the blood and retreat in fear. We are covered by covenant.

Let the blood of Jesus be seen in our stewardship, our giving, and our declarations. We sow in faith and reap in peace. No weapon formed against our provision shall prosper. The destroyer may roam, but he cannot touch what the blood has sealed. Our finances are guarded by the same power that broke Pharaoh's grip.

In Jesus' name, Amen.

DAY 24

GOD DELIGHTS IN MY PROSPERITY

"Let those who favor my righteous cause shout for joy and be glad. Yes, let them say continually, 'Yahweh be magnified, who has pleasure in the prosperity of his servant!'"
— Psalm 35:27 WEB

Jehovah, my Rewarder, I declare that You are pleased when I prosper—not by greed, but by covenant. You take delight in blessing the work of my hands because I honor You with my life and my substance. I am not ashamed to prosper, for it brings You glory.

Let my life become a testimony of divine provision. Let every bill paid, every debt canceled, and every increase received be an echo of Your goodness. My prosperity is not for show—it is for service. I steward wealth to expand Your kingdom, bless the poor, and raise altars to Your name.

Lord, magnify Yourself in my family's finances. Break the ceiling of survival and release us into the realm of overflow. Let our children see what it means to walk with God and lack nothing. Let joy fill our homes as we walk in favor and fulfillment. You are pleased when we flourish, so we boldly receive the fullness of our inheritance.

In Jesus' name, Amen.

DAY 25

DOUBLE FOR MY SHAME

"Instead of your shame you will have double; and instead of dishonor, they will rejoice in their portion. Therefore in their land they will possess double. Everlasting joy will be to them."
— Isaiah 61:7 WEB

O God of restoration, I stand on the power of the blood and decree: every financial shame, every moment of begging, every embarrassment of insufficiency is now being swallowed up in double honor. The blood cries louder than my past. It declares a future of restoration and abundance.

Where I once walked in silence and scarcity, now I shall shout with rejoicing in my portion. You are replacing lack with laughter. No more will I hide my bank statements or fear the knock of collectors. You are crowning me with honor, giving me land, legacy, and laughter. The days of scraping by are over.

Let my family possess the double. Let our name no longer be associated with struggle, but with strength. Our children will inherit not just wealth but wisdom. Where dishonor once lingered, everlasting joy shall now reside. Thank You, Lord, for the blood that qualifies us for more than we deserve.

In Jesus' name, Amen.

DAY 26

CALLING PROVISION INTO BEING

"...calls the things that are not, as though they were."
— Romans 4:17 WEB

El Shaddai, the All-Sufficient One, I step into my blood-bought authority and call forth the provision that is mine in Christ. I do not wait for evidence—I declare the invisible into visibility. I call resources from the north, south, east, and west. I speak to empty accounts, barren fields, and dormant dreams, and I command them to arise!

By the power of the blood, I do not speak as a victim—I decree as a vessel of divine authority. I command provision to align with Your promise. I speak clients into my business, favor into my workplace, solutions into my challenges, and wealth into my hands. Heaven backs my words because they are rooted in covenant.

Let my family speak likewise. Let our mouths be filled with faith, not fear. Let our language shift from limitation to expectation. The blood has opened the gates of supply, and now we walk through with confident declarations. Provision is not just coming—it is here, because You have said so.

In Jesus' name, Amen.

DAY 27

CLEANSED FOR COVENANT ACCESS

"These are those who came out of the great suffering. They washed their robes, and made them white in the Lamb's blood."
— Revelation 7:14 WEB

Holy Redeemer, I praise You for the blood that washes me clean—not just for salvation but for supernatural access. Because of the Lamb's blood, I approach the throne not with guilt, but with grace. I am cleansed, clothed, and qualified to walk in divine prosperity.

Let every stain of financial failure be removed. Let every memory of shame be erased. I am no longer marked by my mistakes—I am marked by mercy. I stand robed in white, ready to receive every blessing written in my name from before time began. Nothing disqualifies me when the blood has justified me.

My family walks in the same cleansing. We are a household of favor, dignity, and wealth—not because of works, but because of the finished work. We do not disqualify ourselves—we step into our access. Let the clean robe of covenant favor shine on our lives and attract every divine connection we need.

In Jesus' name, Amen.

DAY 28

Eternal Redemption, Eternal Provision

"...but through his own blood, entered in once for all into
the Holy Place, having obtained eternal redemption."
— Hebrews 9:12 WEB

Lord Jesus, Eternal Lamb of God, You didn't just redeem me for a
moment—you obtained eternal redemption. And with that eternal
redemption comes eternal provision. I am not subject to the ups
and downs of the world system. I live under the unchanging flow of
Your finished work.

Let the power of this eternal covenant secure my household. Our
provision is not seasonal—it is secured. Our prosperity is not
circumstantial—it is covenantal. Because You entered once for all,
I receive once for all. My needs are met not just for today, but for
every tomorrow. My family will never beg bread because we are
eternally redeemed.

May our lives reflect the security of Your blood. We do not hoard—
we honor. We do not panic—we praise. You have obtained
redemption that cannot be revoked, and from that redemption
flows prosperity that cannot be blocked. Thank You for securing
our future in blood.

In Jesus' name, Amen.

DAY 29

ABUNDANCE BY COVENANT RIGHT

"The Lord will grant you abundant prosperity—in the
fruit of your womb, the young of your livestock and the
crops of your ground—in the land he swore to your
ancestors to give you."
— Deuteronomy 28:11 WEB

O Faithful Covenant God, You swore by Yourself to bless us, and
through the blood of Jesus, we are now partakers of that oath. I
declare that abundance is my covenant right—not a wish, not a
dream, but a guaranteed inheritance ratified in blood.

Let my household be fruitful. Let our work multiply. Let our ground
yield increase. I thank You that every area of my life is touched by
the abundance You promised: our children are thriving, our
income is growing, our legacy is increasing. We prosper in every
season because we are planted in promise.

Let my family carry the evidence of this truth. Let our lives provoke
the world to ask, "What God do you serve?" We are not self-
made—we are covenant-kept. We do not trust in the systems of
man—we trust in the blood-sealed promise of a God who never
fails.

In Jesus' name, Amen.

DAY 30

BOUND BY THE BLOOD TO PROVIDE

"Moses took the blood, and sprinkled it on the people, and said, 'Behold, the blood of the covenant, which Yahweh has made with you concerning all these words.'"
— Exodus 24:8 WEB

Father of the Covenant, I stand sprinkled by the blood that binds You to Your word. You have sworn by the blood that You will provide, protect, and promote. I hold You to Your Word—not with arrogance, but with honor. Your Word is Your bond, and the blood is the seal.

Let the provisions written in Scripture be manifested in my life. Let every "you shall be the head and not the tail" become flesh in my family. Let every "you shall lend and not borrow" be lived out in my finances. The blood has made these words unbreakable.

I bind my household to the Word through the blood. We shall not be moved. We shall not be shaken. We are people of the covenant, and therefore, provision is our portion. Thank You, Lord, for swearing Yourself to our supply. We live in the blessing that cannot be revoked.

In Jesus' name, Amen.

DAY 31

MULTIPLIED THROUGH COVENANT OBEDIENCE

"I will bless you greatly, and I will multiply your offspring greatly like the stars of the heavens, and like the sand which is on the seashore."
— Genesis 22:17 WEB

Lord, Covenant-Keeping God of Abraham, I declare that the blood of Jesus has brought me into the lineage of blessing and multiplied increase. Just as You honored Abraham's obedience with unstoppable multiplication, I stand today under the same covenant, sealed by better blood, and I receive the blessing of increase over my life and my family.

Because of Christ's sacrifice, I step into exponential growth—spiritual, financial, generational. Let my obedience unlock divine strategy and provision. Let every act of faith on my part yield a harvest too numerous to count. You are not a man that You should lie; Your promise to bless and multiply is as alive now as it was on that mountain.

Father, multiply my seed sown, my opportunities, and my influence. Let my children walk in legacy and not labor. I break every ceiling of limitation and receive the Abrahamic blessing through Jesus' obedience on the Cross. My household will increase, our hands will prosper, and our name will be associated with generational wealth—because we obey and believe the covenant.

In Jesus' name, Amen.

DAY 32

OVERCOMING FINANCIAL WARFARE

"They overcame him because of the Lamb's blood, and
because of the word of their testimony."
— Revelation 12:11 WEB

Victorious Lord, I declare that every financial battle waged against
my life and household is now subdued under the blood of the
Lamb. By the authority of the blood and the power of my testimony,
I overcome every demonic resistance, every devourer, and every
sabotage assigned to my increase.

The blood of Jesus testifies louder than debt, louder than scarcity,
louder than generational curses. I silence the voice of lack and rise
in the triumph of covenant victory. I am not a victim—I am a
blood-covered overcomer. Let the roar of the redeemed echo
through my finances and household, causing every enemy to flee.

Father, let every attack on our harvest be reversed. Let angels of
provision war on our behalf. My family walks in victory—we do
not retreat. Our wealth is not fragile, our blessing is not vulnerable.
The enemy may come in one way, but by the blood, he flees in seven.
In Jesus' name, Amen.

DAY 33

No Sorrow in My Blessing

"The Lord's blessing brings wealth, and he adds no trouble to it."
— Proverbs 10:22 WEB

Faithful Provider, I praise You for the blessing that enriches without anxiety. I reject toil without fruit and embrace wealth that comes from Your hand alone. The blessing of the Lord is upon me through the blood of Jesus, and I declare that sorrow and striving shall have no place in my prosperity.

Every heavy yoke of financial stress is broken. I step into rest-driven results, not hustle-induced hardship. You give me power to get wealth without it draining my peace. Your blessing is complete—it brings joy, not burdens; honor, not shame.

Lord, let my family walk in this blessing. Let laughter fill our home instead of worry. May our financial story glorify You, not our efforts. I declare a divine distinction: we prosper without compromise, without corners cut, without sleepless striving. The blood has opened the door, and we walk through it joyfully.

In Jesus' name, Amen.

DAY 34

SUPERNATURAL PROVISION WITHOUT CURRENCY

"Come, everyone who thirsts, to the waters! Come, he
who has no money, buy, and eat!"
— Isaiah 55:1 WEB

Holy Source of All, I lift my hands to receive the supply that does
not require natural currency. I come to the well of grace, to the
marketplace of mercy, where Your blood has already paid my price.
I buy without money and eat without debt. I receive supernatural
provision by faith.

Let divine resources flow into my life and family. Let doors open
that no man can explain. You are not limited by economy, by
account balance, or by human systems. I live in the reality of grace
economics—where You supply all my needs according to the riches
of glory, not the poverty of circumstance.

Lord, let my household be marked by miracles. Provide what we
didn't earn. Deliver what we didn't pay for. Let us testify of how we
received more than we asked, simply because we believed. We feast
where others famine, we rise where others fall—because we live by
grace, not gold.

In Jesus' name, Amen.

DAY 35

SATISFACTION IN EVERY FAMINE

"They shall not be disappointed in the time of evil. In the
days of famine they shall be satisfied."
— Psalm 37:19 WEB

God of Unfailing Supply, I declare that no season can rob me of
provision. Though the world may fear famine, I walk in blood-
backed satisfaction. You are my Source, and in You, my family is
never forsaken. Even in scarcity, we thrive. Even in drought, we
drink.

I break the grip of recession over my household. I cancel every
agreement with fear and speak abundance into every barren place.
In times of shaking, You establish me. While others store up in fear,
I sow in faith and reap in peace.

Let satisfaction reign in our home. Let our children never know
lack. May our pantry, our accounts, and our joy remain full—proof
that we are the Lord's. Thank You for being our Shepherd in the
storm and our Table-setter in the wilderness.

In Jesus' name, Amen.

DAY 36

Overflow in All Things

"God is able to make all grace abound to you, that you, always having all sufficiency in everything, may abound to every good work."
— 2 Corinthians 9:8 WEB

All-Sufficient King, I lift my voice in gratitude for the overflow secured by the blood. You are able—and I believe. I declare over my life and family: we will never lack for anything necessary to do Your will. Grace abounds, and sufficiency is our standard.

Every area of insufficiency is now flooded with grace. You've equipped me to be a vessel of generosity, not just survival. We abound to every good work. We give, sow, build, bless—because You keep filling and refilling us. The more we pour, the more You provide.

Father, let this grace touch my entire household. Let us become a well that never runs dry. We operate in overflow—not just for ourselves but for the mission You've assigned us. The blood has guaranteed access, and we walk in the abundance of Your ability, not our own.

In Jesus' name, Amen.

DAY 37

No More Guilt, Only Grace

"For this is my blood of the new covenant, which is poured
out for many for the remission of sins."
— Matthew 26:28 WEB

Redeeming Savior, I rejoice in the blood that has forever erased my
guilt. Every trace of sin, shame, and unworthiness has been washed
away. I am no longer disqualified. I am righteous by the blood, and
therefore, prosperity can no longer be hindered.

I break agreement with every lie that says I don't deserve
abundance. The blood says I'm clean. The Cross says I'm worthy. I
reject condemnation and walk in holy confidence. My financial
increase is not based on perfection—it's rooted in the remission of
sin.

Let my family live free—free from the shame of past mistakes, free
from the fear of judgment, free to prosper with joy. We walk boldly
into the inheritance Jesus died to give us. The stain is gone. The
door is open. The blessing flows freely.

In Jesus' name, Amen.

DAY 38

ABRAHAMIC WEALTH FLOWS TO ME

"Abram was very rich in livestock, in silver, and in gold."
— Genesis 13:2 WEB

God of Abraham, Isaac, and Jacob, I declare that I am a child of the covenant. What flowed to Abraham now flows to me through the blood of Jesus. I step into covenant wealth—not by lineage of the flesh, but by the lineage of faith.

Make my household rich—not just in possessions, but in purpose. Let silver and gold serve the mission. Let our wealth be proof of Your faithfulness. You made Abraham rich, and You've not changed. What You did then, You do now—through the better covenant sealed in Christ's blood.

I refuse to settle for less than what You promised. I receive land, legacy, and livestock in whatever form it takes today—properties, businesses, influence, and divine ideas. Let my children grow up in the atmosphere of abundance. Let our family story echo the testimony of Abraham.

In Jesus' name, Amen.

DAY 39

EQUIPPED FOR PROSPERITY

"Now may the God of peace... through the blood of the
eternal covenant... make you complete in every good
work, to do his will..."
— Hebrews 13:20–21 WEB

God of Peace and Purpose, I thank You for the blood of the eternal
covenant that equips me with everything needed for abundance. I
am not lacking—I am complete. I have everything I need to walk
in divine prosperity and to fulfill my assignment.

Make me skilled in stewardship, strong in wisdom, and sharp in
discernment. Equip my family to carry the weight of blessing
without being crushed. Let every good work be supplied—nothing
missing, nothing broken. Through the blood, You've not only
redeemed me, but resourced me.

May the work of our hands prosper because Your hand is upon us.
Let our lives reflect the completeness that comes from You alone.
We lack no good thing, because we serve a good God. Through the
eternal blood covenant, we are empowered for eternal results.

In Jesus' name, Amen.

DAY 40

My Year is Crowned

"You crown the year with your bounty. Your carts overflow
with abundance."
— Psalm 65:11 WEB

Lord of the Harvest, I decree that this is the year of divine
abundance. You have crowned it—marked it, blessed it, and filled
it with Your goodness. I step into each month with faith, each day
with favor, and each hour with expectancy. Your carts overflow, and
I ride in the river of Your plenty.

Let every month bring fruit. Let every season produce joy. My
family will not survive the year—we will thrive in it. Your blood has
already purchased the blessing, and we simply walk in it. No more
begging. No more barrenness. The year has been crowned.

I speak over my household: this year, we will see increase like never
before. Projects will prosper, debts will dissolve, ideas will ignite.
We will eat in plenty and praise the name of the Lord. The blood is
speaking, and it speaks overflow.

In Jesus' name, Amen.

DAY 41

DAYS IN PROSPERITY, YEARS IN PLEASURE

"If they listen and serve him, they shall spend their days
in prosperity, and their years in pleasures."
— Job 36:11 WEB

Majestic Father, I step into the promise of covenant prosperity through the obedience You empower. I don't labor under obligation, I walk in joyful surrender. My ears are tuned to Your voice, and my heart is ready to follow. Because I listen and serve You, I lay claim to days filled with abundance and years filled with joy.

Let every area of my life—my health, my home, my business, my finances, and my family—come into alignment with the decree of this Word. May our household be a testimony that obedience is not a burden but a blessed pathway to overflow. As I serve You with integrity, You crown my life with satisfaction.

Let my children live in the fruit of my yieldedness. Let their days be long and their paths be straight. We are not trapped in toil—we are tethered to Your goodness. I reject every lie that says prosperity is for others. I declare: our family will spend our days in prosperity, and our years in pleasures, because we walk in covenant obedience.

In Jesus' name, Amen.

DAY 42

PROSPER IN ALL YOU DO

"Keep therefore the words of this covenant and do them,
that you may prosper in all that you do."
— Deuteronomy 29:9 WEB

Faithful Covenant-Keeper, I declare that my life is built on the blood-bought promises of Your Word. I choose today to honor and keep the covenant not by my strength, but by the Spirit's power. I receive the grace to walk in Your ways so that I may prosper in all that I do.

Let nothing in my life be untouched by this promise. Let my decisions prosper, my relationships prosper, my parenting prosper, my career prosper, and my household flourish. Because of the covenant, prosperity is not just a possibility—it is my portion. I reject smallness and failure, and I embrace Your grace for total life prosperity.

Let my family be known as a people who do well because they live well with You. Let the fruit of this covenant show up in our finances, our dreams, and the works of our hands. Prosperity is not a random occurrence—it is the inevitable result of covenant alignment. I walk in this promise with confidence.

In Jesus' name, Amen.

DAY 43

Open the Windows of Heaven

"Bring the whole tithe into the storehouse... I will open the
windows of heaven for you, and pour you out a blessing..."
— Malachi 3:10 WEB

God of Overflow, I lift my eyes to the heavens and declare: my
obedience unlocks the storehouses of abundance. I bring my tithe
not out of duty but out of devotion, because the blood has already
secured every promise for me. I do not operate under a curse—I
live under an open heaven.

Open the windows of heaven over my life and family. Let what You
pour out be so rich, so vast, so undeniable that there is not room
enough to contain it. Let resources come from expected and
unexpected places. Let favor locate us. Let our barns overflow and
our jars never run dry.

I reject the famine mindset. I walk in the economy of heaven, which
is fueled by faith and activated by covenant. I am not surviving—
I'm thriving. My family will never lack. Our needs are met. Our
dreams are funded. Our legacy is secure because we honor You with
what is Yours.

In Jesus' name, Amen.

DAY 44

FREEDOM FROM FINANCIAL CAPTIVITY

"As for you also, because of the blood of your covenant, I
have set free your prisoners from the pit in which is no
water."
— Zechariah 9:11 WEB

Blood-Sealing Deliverer, I declare that every chain of financial
captivity over my life and family is broken by the blood of the
covenant. You have seen our prison, You have heard our cry, and
You have moved with power to set us free from every cycle of lack
and limitation.

I speak freedom over every debt, every lingering financial bondage,
and every generational curse of poverty. The pit is dry, but the blood
is living! We are not stuck—we are released! I prophesy that we are
coming out of financial struggle and stepping into surplus. The
blood has spoken, and the pit must let go.

My family will no longer be imprisoned by scarcity, fear, or survival.
We will walk in the liberty of those whose needs are met and whose
futures are secure. Because of the blood, we are not only free—we
are fruitful. What once held us will now serve as a platform for
praise.

In Jesus' name, Amen.

DAY 45

TREASURES IN SECRET PLACES

"I will give you the treasures of darkness, and hidden riches of secret places..."
— Isaiah 45:3 WEB

O God who reveals mysteries, I stand in awe of the hidden wealth You've prepared for those who walk in covenant. You do not just give bread—you reveal buried treasure. You do not just meet needs—you unveil supernatural provision stored in secret places.

I receive revelation today to see what others overlook. Open my eyes to opportunities, strategies, partnerships, and ideas that unlock prosperity for my life and household. Let every secret treasure assigned to my name come into my possession. I declare that nothing hidden shall stay hidden from the righteous.

Let my family walk in the wisdom of divine discovery. Let us possess what was stored for us. We will not live off crumbs when You've prepared treasure. What was hidden is now revealed. What was buried is now released. Because I am blood-covered, I walk with covenant insight to access what the world cannot see.

In Jesus' name, Amen.

DAY 46

WHATEVER I DO WILL PROSPER

"He will be like a tree planted by the streams of water...
whatever he does shall prosper."
— Psalm 1:3 WEB

Rooted and Fruitful God, I plant myself today by the waters of Your
Word and covenant. I declare that I am not a wandering branch—
I am a well-watered tree. My roots run deep in the truth of who You
are, and because of that, everything I touch is blessed.

I decree that my efforts are not in vain. Whatever I do—every
project, every meeting, every investment, every plan—shall
prosper. I refuse to be moved by what I see. I stand planted in the
soil of divine supply, and I draw daily from the rivers of
supernatural abundance.

Let my family be trees of prosperity. Let our leaves never wither. Let
our fruit never fail. We are not shaken by drought or storms—we
flourish in every season. This is our covenant position: productive,
prosperous, and planted by the living water of Christ's blood.

In Jesus' name, Amen.

DAY 47

LIFE MORE ABUNDANTLY

"I came that they may have life, and may have it
abundantly."
— John 10:10 WEB

Jesus, Abundant Life-Giver, I receive what You came to give. I do
not settle for mere survival. You did not shed Your blood so I could
barely make it—you gave it that I might have life in overflow. Every
drop of blood You shed was a declaration of abundance for me.

I embrace the full expression of life—spiritually, emotionally,
financially, relationally. My life and the life of my family are marked
by peace, increase, and joy. I break agreement with the thief who
comes to steal, kill, and destroy. We refuse to live beneath the
standard of Your blood-bought promise.

Abundance is not a dream—it is our divine reality. Our table is full,
our oil is fresh, and our joy is complete. You have opened wide the
gates of blessing, and we walk in boldly. The days of lack are over.
We have life, and we have it more abundantly.

In Jesus' name, Amen.

DAY 48

You Alone Are the Source

"Both riches and honor come from you. You rule over all..."
— 1 Chronicles 29:12 WEB

Sovereign King, I lift my hands and heart in total acknowledgment: You alone are the Source of every blessing. Riches don't come from men. Honor doesn't come from effort. They come from You—the One who sits enthroned over all the earth and rules with wisdom and mercy.

Every dollar I possess, every opportunity I receive, every platform I stand on—it all flows from Your hand. I will not worship the gift, but the Giver. I will not idolize the provision, but exalt the Provider. You are the one who elevates, promotes, and multiplies. My family will never forget that it is You who makes us wealthy.

May our home be a place of constant gratitude. Let my children grow up declaring, "God is our Source." I reject pride and self-dependence. I root myself in reverence and surrender. May our abundance point the world back to You—the One from whom all blessings flow.

In Jesus' name, Amen.

DAY 49

Expecting Every Good Thing

"He who didn't spare his own Son, but delivered him up
for us all, how would he not also with him freely give us all
things?"
— Romans 8:32 WEB

Gracious Father, if You gave Your very best—Your own Son—how
could I ever doubt Your willingness to bless me with all things? I
stand in awe of Your generosity and boldly expect every good thing
to manifest in my life and family, not by entitlement, but by blood-
bought grace.

I refuse to think small or settle for less. You have given all—so I
expect all. Peace, joy, abundance, wisdom, increase—it's all
included in the package of redemption. My eyes are lifted, my faith
is alive, and my heart is open to receive without fear or hesitation.

Let my family live with holy expectation. Let our language shift
from "maybe" to "surely." We live under the shadow of the cross,
and in that shadow there is no lack. We don't have to strive for what
You delight to give. We receive it all with open hands.

In Jesus' name, Amen.

DAY 50

No Good Thing Withheld

"For Yahweh God is a sun and a shield. Yahweh will give grace and glory. He withholds no good thing from those who walk blamelessly."
— Psalm 84:11 WEB

Radiant Sun and Faithful Shield, I bless Your name for the light You shine on my path and the protection You give to my life. You are both Provider and Defender. You don't just give grace—you give glory. And because of the blood, I walk blameless before You, expecting nothing to be withheld.

You withhold no good thing. Not one. If it's good and godly, You delight to release it. I reject every thought that says You are holding back. I rebuke the lie that says I must beg for Your favor. You are my covenant Father, and You rejoice in my well-being.

Let my family walk in this truth with boldness. Every home, every career, every prayer, every plan—let it be touched by the abundance You release. We will not live beneath the blessing. We will live as those who are wrapped in grace and saturated in goodness.

In Jesus' name, Amen.

DAY 51

BLOOD-MARK ON MY LABOR

"Yahweh was with Joseph, and he was a prosperous man.
He was in the house of his master the Egyptian. His master
saw that Yahweh was with him, and that Yahweh made all
that he did prosper in his hand."
— Genesis 39:2–3 WEB

Lord, my Covenant Partner, I declare that the same blood that redeemed my soul also rests upon the work of my hands. Just as You caused Joseph to prosper in a strange land, so I decree that everything I touch—my job, my business, my investments—is marked for increase because of Your presence and favor.

I thank You that because of the blood of Jesus, my labor is not in vain. I am not bound by economic systems or company politics—I operate under the influence of divine success. Let those around me see Your hand on my life. Let my results provoke recognition, honor, and reward. The blood of Jesus is my seal of excellence, productivity, and unstoppable advancement.

May this same covenant blessing rest on my family. Let every endeavor of my spouse and children flourish. Let our house be filled with testimonies of supernatural results and undeniable prosperity. We are not common—we are covenant-marked. And because the blood is on our hands, our labor will always yield more than enough.

In Jesus' name, Amen.

DAY 52

HONORING THE BLOOD GUARANTEE

"How much worse punishment do you think he will be
judged worthy of, who has trodden under foot the Son of
God, and has counted the blood of the covenant with
which he was sanctified an unholy thing..."
— Hebrews 10:29 WEB

O Holy and Righteous God, I exalt the blood of the covenant that
has sanctified me and guaranteed my access to divine abundance. I
will not treat lightly what You have sealed with the highest price—
Your Son's life. I honor the blood that speaks of better things:
increase, favor, and overflow.

I declare that my provision is not a random occurrence but a right
secured by the blood of Jesus. I am not at the mercy of
circumstances; I live under a divine guarantee. Let heaven record
today that I esteem the covenant. I believe it, I receive it, and I live
by it. I will not reduce prosperity to chance or toil—it is the fruit of
the covenant.

Let this reverence extend to my household. Let my family be known
for honoring the blood, and let our lives reflect the wealth, peace,
and security found in it. We are not beggars—we are believers. And
the covenant we honor will overflow into every area of our lives.

In Jesus' name, Amen.

DAY 53

TREASURED AND POSITIONED BY FAVOR

"Now therefore, if you will indeed obey my voice and keep
my covenant, then you shall be my own possession from
among all peoples, for all the earth is mine."
— Exodus 19:5 WEB

Majestic King, I praise You for making me—and my household—
Your treasured possession through the blood of Jesus. You have
chosen me out of all the earth, not because of my merit but because
of mercy. I receive this favor not as flattery, but as fact, rooted in
covenant truth.

You have positioned me for influence, placed me in strategic
locations, and surrounded me with divine opportunities. I am not
wandering—I am appointed. I am not invisible—I am set apart.
Through the blood, I am qualified to dwell in places others only
dream of, and to receive what others labor for without access.

Let this positioning extend to my family. May my children walk into
divine assignments and favor-packed destinies. May my spouse
receive honor and recognition in every sphere. We are not
hidden—we are highlighted by heaven. And because we are
treasured by the Most High, we shall never live beneath our
inheritance.

In Jesus' name, Amen.

DAY 54

OVERTAKEN BY COVENANT BLESSINGS

"All these blessings will come upon you, and overtake you,
if you listen to Yahweh your God's voice."
— Deuteronomy 28:2 WEB

Covenant-Keeping God, I open my life to be overtaken—not by trouble, not by fear, but by blessing. You have spoken, and I believe: because of the blood, I have the right to be pursued by Your promises. I decree that I don't chase blessings—blessings chase me.

Let favor follow me into every room. Let provision meet me before I know I need it. Let contracts, open doors, and divine connections overtake me, not by manipulation but by manifestation of covenant. I align my heart to Your voice, and the blessings flow without striving.

May my family be swept into this divine overtaking. Let our children be surrounded by good success. Let every generation run ahead of curses and straight into blessings. Because of the covenant, we live not at the back—but at the front of heaven's favor.

In Jesus' name, Amen.

DAY 55

TAUGHT TO PROFIT BY THE LORD

"I am Yahweh your God, who teaches you to profit, who
leads you by the way you should go."
— Isaiah 48:17 WEB

Holy Instructor of Increase, I submit my mind and my plans to You.
You are the God who teaches me to profit. You do not delight in
waste or poverty, but You guide me into abundance, one strategy,
one idea, one step at a time. The blood gives me access to divine
instruction.

Open my ears to wisdom that multiplies wealth. Lead me in paths
that turn effort into harvest. Give me supernatural insight for my
business, career, and finances. I reject worldly striving—I embrace
Spirit-led strategies. I am not led by trends—I am led by truth.

Let this anointing rest on my family. May my household be known
for wise stewardship and innovative solutions. Let our table
overflow not just with bread, but with brilliance. We are taught of
the Lord, and therefore, we cannot help but prosper.

In Jesus' name, Amen.

DAY 56

God's Investment Must Prosper

"Take heed, therefore, to yourselves...to shepherd the assembly of the Lord and God which he purchased with his own blood."
— Acts 20:28 WEB

Righteous Redeemer, You have purchased my life—not with silver or gold, but with Your own blood. I am not cheap, not forgotten, not random—I am Your costly investment. And because You paid the highest price, I know You will ensure that I prosper, fulfill purpose, and bring You glory.

I will not treat my life as common. I am a divine asset, bought for impact. Let my days produce fruit, my efforts yield results, and my walk reflect worth. I refuse to squander what heaven has paid dearly for. I arise today with dignity, responsibility, and authority.

Let my family walk in this same revelation. May we never underestimate ourselves or each other. May our value be seen in how we speak, live, and serve. We are Your possession, paid in full, and You will ensure that Your investment bears eternal return.

In Jesus' name, Amen.

DAY 57

BARNS FILLED, VATS OVERFLOWING

"So your barns will be filled with plenty, and your vats will
overflow with new wine."
— Proverbs 3:10 WEB

Lord of the Harvest, I receive Your promise today: my barns shall
be filled, and my vats shall overflow. By the covenant blood of Jesus,
I declare that I am not meant for just enough—I am destined for
overflow. My storage will not be empty, and my supply will not run
dry.

Because I honor You with my substance, I receive the fullness of
Your Word. Let every account, every business, every project in my
hand be filled with divine provision. Let new wine—fresh
opportunities, fresh creativity, fresh resources—overflow into
every area of my life.

I speak the same over my family. We do not live from paycheck to
paycheck—we live from provision to provision. Our barns are full,
our homes are blessed, and our joy is complete. We are stewards of
the overflow, because the blood has made room for more.

In Jesus' name, Amen.

DAY 58

Increase Upon Increase

"May Yahweh increase you more and more, you and your children."
— Psalm 115:14 WEB

God of Increase, I thank You for the blood of Jesus that unlocks generational multiplication. I declare that my life is not stagnant. I am increasing—more and more. Not just me, but my children after me. The covenant speaks multiplication, and I receive it now.

Let every area of my life rise to new levels: my income, my wisdom, my influence, my opportunities. I am not diminishing—I am enlarging. I declare that the cycle of decrease is broken. I expect growth because I am joined to a God who cannot fail.

Let my family be swept into this divine current. May our children go further, rise higher, and shine brighter. May every generation outdo the last in wisdom, wealth, and worship. You are the God of more and more, and we say yes to the increase.

In Jesus' name, Amen.

DAY 59

HARVEST FROM BLOOD-BOUGHT SEED

"Don't be deceived. God is not mocked, for whatever a
man sows, that he will also reap."
— Galatians 6:7 WEB

Covenant God, I declare today that every seed I have sown is
returning with increase. You are not unjust, and You do not forget.
The blood of Jesus has marked my seed, protected it, and
guaranteed its harvest. What I sow in faith, I shall reap in fullness.

I sow my time, my tithes, my service, my obedience—and I declare,
by blood covenant, that my harvest is inevitable. I reject fear and
embrace faith. I call forth every delayed harvest. I summon every
seed sown in tears to return with joy.

Let my family walk in this revelation. Let every act of kindness,
every offering, every sacrifice made in faith come back pressed
down, shaken together, and running over. We are not sowing in
vain. The blood has blessed our ground.

In Jesus' name, Amen.

DAY 60

FINAL INHERITANCE, FULLY SECURED

"He said to me, 'I am the Alpha and the Omega, the Beginning and the End. I will give freely to him who is thirsty from the spring of the water of life. He who overcomes, I will give him these things. I will be his God, and he will be my son.'"
— Revelation 21:6–7 WEB

Alpha and Omega, my Beginning and my End, I worship You for the inheritance You've secured by Your blood. You have not left me to wander—I have a guaranteed future. I thirst for You, and You fill me with life, purpose, and eternal reward.

I declare that I am an overcomer. Every battle I face is already settled in Christ. I don't just survive—I inherit. The spring of life flows through me and into everything I touch. My inheritance is not in man's hands—it is sealed in heaven and revealed in the earth.

Let my household walk in this final assurance. We are sons and daughters of God, destined to overcome and receive what the blood has paid for. We are heirs of every promise, partakers of every blessing, and recipients of every reward.

In Jesus' name, Amen.

Epilogue

As you close out this 60-day journey, remember: covenant prosperity is not an event—it's a lifestyle. The prayers you've prayed were not just for a season, but for a new way of living. God has positioned you, by the blood of Jesus, to become a channel of His wealth, a steward of His provision, and a witness of His abundance in the earth.

You may still be walking through process, but the seed has been sown. Keep declaring what the blood declares. Keep honoring God with your increase. Keep expecting more, not because of greed, but because of grace. The Cross didn't just cancel sin—it released supply. And that supply is now your birthright.

Go forward in faith. Sow generously. Receive boldly. And above all, remember: your prosperity brings God pleasure and advances His kingdom. Walk in it daily—with confidence, integrity, and joy.

ENCOURAGE OTHERS WITH YOUR STORY

If this prayer guide has strengthened your faith, deepened your intercession, or helped you stand in the gap, would you consider leaving a short review on Amazon? Your feedback not only encourages others but also helps more believers discover this resource and join in the prayer movement. Every review—just a few sentences—makes a difference and helps spread the call to command the evening. Thank you for being part of this movement.

More from PrayerScripts

Pardon Through the Blood:

60 Days of Prayers for Total Forgiveness and Freedom

Guilt is a prison. The blood of Jesus holds the key.

Pardon Through the Blood invites you on a 60-day journey into the liberating power of Christ's sacrifice—a sacred cleansing that reaches deeper than shame, regret, or condemnation. If you've ever felt stuck in cycles of failure, haunted by your past, or burdened by hidden sin, this book is your roadmap to lasting forgiveness and spiritual freedom. Each day offers a blood-specific Scripture, a focused prayer theme, and a prophetic, Spirit-filled prayer that will help you boldly approach God's mercy seat. You'll experience what it means to be fully forgiven, deeply cleansed, and restored to right relationship with the Father—all through the blood of Jesus.

PROTECTION THROUGH THE BLOOD:

60 DAYS OF PRAYERS FOR LIVING UNTOUCHABLE UNDER CHRIST'S BLOOD

You are not helpless. You are not exposed. You are covered—completely—by the blood of Jesus.

In a world of rising dangers, demonic assaults, and spiritual unpredictability, Protection Through the Blood equips you and your family to live untouchable under the supernatural shield of Christ's blood. Every day's entry is a power-packed prayer experience rooted in Scripture—designed to build a blood-line barrier around your life, home, and destiny.. Part of *The Blood Covenant Series,* this second volume is a must-have companion for believers who refuse to live defenseless in a dark world. If you're ready to activate heaven's strongest defense system and stand boldly in the shadow of the Almighty, this 60-day journey is for you.

Live bold. Live covered. Live untouchable—through the blood.

PREVAIL THROUGH THE BLOOD:

60 DAYS OF PRAYERS FOR SPIRITUAL MASTERY OVER THE ENEMY

What if every scheme of the enemy against your life could be dismantled—by one unstoppable weapon?

In *Prevail Through the Blood*, you'll discover how to wield the most powerful force in the universe—the Blood of Jesus Christ—to overcome every spiritual assault, shatter generational yokes, and walk in daily victory. This is more than a prayer book. It is your 60-day spiritual war manual, designed to train your hands for battle and your heart for triumph. This third installment in The Blood Covenant Series invites you into a journey of spiritual mastery. Whether you are in the heat of battle or standing in victory, every page will sharpen your discernment, stir your faith, and saturate your home in the protective power of Christ's blood.

Break free from every chain. Pray with fire. Win with the Blood.

PRESERVATION THROUGH THE BLOOD:

60 DAYS OF PRAYERS FOR DIVINE HEALING AND WHOLENESS

Unlock Lasting Healing and Wholeness Through the Blood of Jesus

Preservation Through the Blood: 60 Days of Prayers for Divine Healing and Wholeness is your prophetic, Scripture-packed guide to receiving total restoration in your body, soul, and spirit through the covenant power of Christ's blood. More than a devotional, this book is a healing altar—built on 60 carefully selected Bible verses that directly reveal God's will to heal and preserve you.

Whether you're battling chronic illness, emotional trauma, lingering symptoms, or generational afflictions, these blood-based prayers will speak directly to the root of the issue to appropriate divine healing. This book equips you to confront the source, not just the symptoms.

COMMAND YOUR MORNING: 30 DAYS OF PRAYERS AND DECLARATIONS TO SEIZE YOUR DAY AND SHAPE YOUR DESTINY

There is a battle over every morning—and every believer must choose to either drift into the day or command it.

Command Your Morning: 30 Days of Prayers and Declarations to Seize Your Day and Shape Your Destiny is a spiritually charged guide to help you start each day with purpose, power, and prophetic clarity. This is more than a devotional—it's a call to action. Each day in this 30-day journey is built around **five core biblical themes** that set the spiritual tone for your day: **Praise, Purpose, Protection, Provision** and **Position.** Don't just wake up. Command your morning—and shape your destiny.

COMMAND YOUR NIGHT: 30 DAYS OF PRAYERS AND DECLARATIONS TO SECURE YOUR REST AND SHAPE YOUR TOMORROW

Every night is a spiritual battlefield—what you do before you sleep can determine the course of your tomorrow.

Command Your Night: 30 Days of Prayers and Declarations to Secure Your Rest and Shape Your Tomorrow is a powerful devotional prayer manual designed to help you end each day in victory, not vulnerability. Whether you're battling anxiety, spiritual attacks, restlessness, or simply longing for deeper peace, this book equips you to reclaim your night with bold, Scripture-rooted prayers. Each night is structured around five strategic prayer themes: *Shut, Shield, Silence, Show, Sleep.*

COMMAND YOUR EVENING: 30 DAYS OF PRAYERS AND
DECLARATIONS TO RELEASE THE DAY AND RECLAIM INTIMACY WITH GOD

There is a battle over every transition—and evening is one of the most spiritually neglected.

Command Your Evening is the third book in the **Command Your Destiny** series—following *Command Your Morning* and *Command Your Night*. In heaven's rhythm, the evening is not just a wind-down—it's a window. A sacred hour where destinies are recalibrated, burdens are lifted, and hearts are re-centered in the presence of God. In *Command Your Evening*, you'll journey through 30 days of intentional, Spirit-led prayers and prophetic declarations centered around five key evening themes: **Release, Renew, Refocus, Rebuild,** and **Rest.**

SCRIPTURES & PRAYERS FOR DELIVERANCE FROM TROUBLE: 40 DAYS OF PRAYER FOR WHEN LIFE FEELS OVERWHELMING

Are you walking through a season where life feels heavy, hope feels distant, and your prayers feel weak?

Scriptures & Prayers for Deliverance from Trouble is a 40-day journey of honest prayers and powerful Scriptures to help you find peace, strength, and healing when life is overwhelming. Each day offers a personal, Scripture-based prayer written in the language of real faith and raw trust. This devotional isn't about perfect words— it's about real connection with God when you need Him most.

SCRIPTURES & PRAYERS FOR DELIVERANCE FROM EVIL:

50 DAYS OF PRAYER TO OVERCOME DARKNESS AND FIND GOD'S PROTECTION

When darkness presses in, how do you pray?

When fear grips your heart or unseen battles rage around you, you need more than generic words—you need Scripture, truth, and the steady hand of God to lead you through.

Scriptures & Prayers for Deliverance from Evil: 50 Days of Prayer to Overcome Darkness and Find God's Protection is a powerful devotional journey designed to help you pray boldly and biblically through seasons of spiritual warfare, oppression, fear, or uncertainty.

SCRIPTURES & PRAYERS FOR ENGAGING THE ENEMY:

70 DAYS OF PRAYER TO REBUKE THE ENEMY AND RELEASE GOD'S POWER

You weren't called to run from the battle—

you were anointed to win it.

Scriptures & Prayers for Engaging the Enemy: 70 Days of Prayer to Rebuke the Enemy and Release God's Power is a bold devotional for believers who are ready to rise, resist, and reclaim what the enemy has tried to steal. If you're tired of feeling spiritually outnumbered, this book will equip you to fight back—with Scripture in your mouth and power in your prayers. Over 70 days, you'll be guided through five strategic phases of spiritual warfare: (1) Rebuking the Enemy, (2) Releasing Terror Upon the Enemy (3) Praying for the Fall of the Enemy (4) Treading Upon the Enemy (5) When Heaven Strikes.

The war is real. But so is your victory.

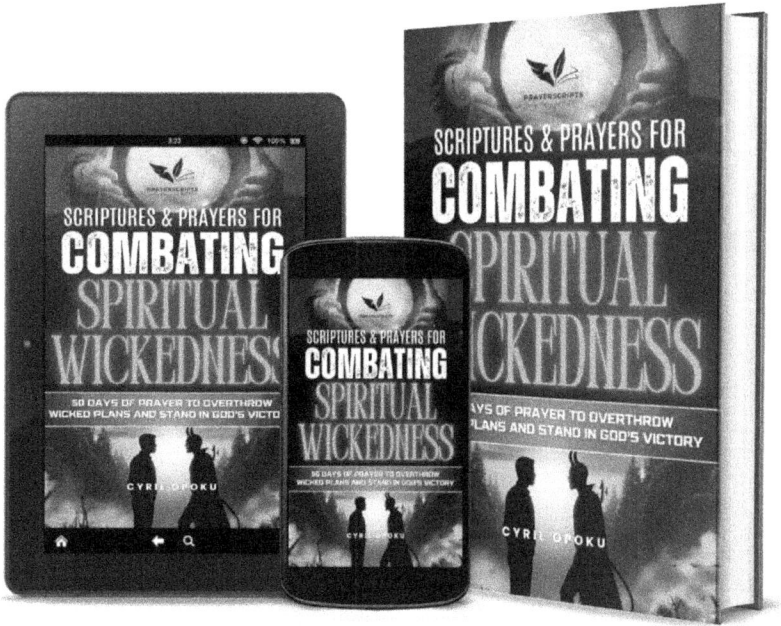

SCRIPTURES & PRAYERS FOR COMBATING SPIRITUAL WICKEDNESS:

50 DAYS OF PRAYER TO OVERTHROW WICKED PLANS AND STAND IN GOD'S VICTORY

Are you facing opposition that feels deeper than the natural? Do you sense hidden resistance working against your progress, peace, or purpose? You're not imagining it—and you're not powerless.

Rooted in the authority of Scripture and fueled by bold, targeted prayers, *Scriptures & Prayers for Combating Spiritual Wickedness* equips you to confront darkness head-on. Each day features a focused Bible passage and a heartfelt, Scripture-based prayer designed to nullify ungodly counsel, disrupt demonic schemes, and establish God's victory in every area of your life.

STANDING IN THE GAP FOR COVENANT AWAKENING:

30 DAYS OF PRAYER FOR NATIONAL REPENTANCE, RIGHTEOUS LEADERSHIP & GOD'S SOVEREIGN RULE

What if your prayers could help turn the tide of a nation?

America stands at a spiritual crossroads. Division deepens, truth is under siege, and righteousness is being redefined. But God is still searching for those who will stand in the gap—intercessors who will cry out for mercy, justice, and national awakening.

Standing in the Gap for Covenant Awakening is a 30-day prayer guide for believers who sense the urgency of the hour and long to see their nation return to God.

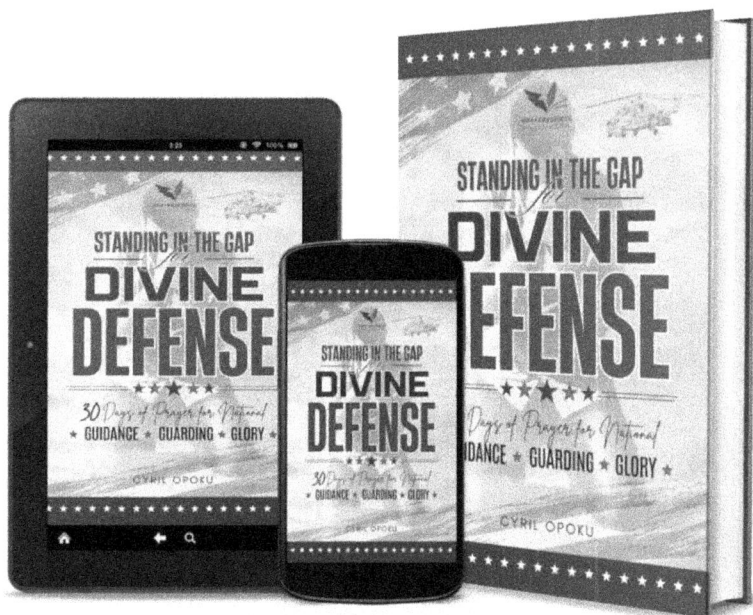

STANDING IN THE GAP FOR DIVINE DEFENSE:

30 DAYS OF PRAYER FOR NATIONAL GUIDANCE, GUARDING & GLORY

When the foundations of a nation feel as if they're shaking, prayer is the strongest fortress you can build.

Standing in the Gap for Divine Defense: 30 Days of Prayer for National Guidance, Guarding & Glory is your call to action—a 30-day journey of powerful, Scripture-rooted intercession that invites everyday believers to become watchmen on the walls for their nation. Drawing on timeless truths from God's Word, this devotional equips you to stand in the gap for your nation and **Seek Heaven's Wisdom, Secure Divine Protection,** and **Ignite Spiritual Awakening.** If you sense the urgency of the hour and long to see your country guided and guarded by the hand of God, open these pages. Stand in the gap. Watch Him move.

STANDING IN THE GAP FOR NATIONAL HEALING:

40 DAYS OF PRAYER FOR RECONCILIATION, RIGHTEOUSNESS, AND RESTORATION

What if your prayers could help heal a nation? What if God is waiting for someone—like you—to stand in the gap?

Standing in the Gap for National Healing: 40 Days of Prayer for Reconciliation, Righteousness, and Restoration is a bold, Spirit-filled call to action for believers who refuse to sit on the sidelines while their nation drifts further from God. In a time marked by division, confusion, and moral decline, this book equips you to pray with power, precision, and unshakable hope. Inside, you'll find 40 days of Scripture-based intercession divided into three strategic sections: **Peace, Unity & Reconciliation, Morality, Truth & Righteous Leadership**, and **National Restoration & Reformation**. It's time to stop watching history unfold—and start shaping it in prayer.

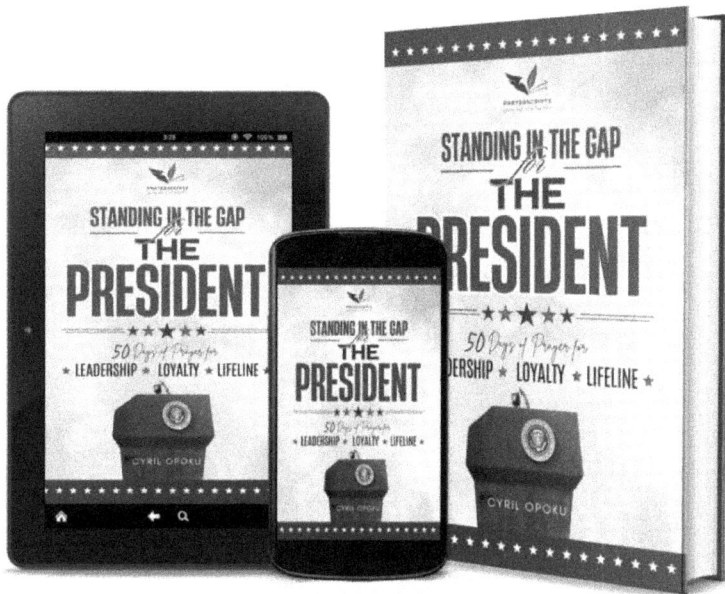

STANDING IN THE GAP FOR THE PRESIDENT:

50 DAYS OF PRAYER FOR LEADERSHIP, LOYALTY, AND LIFELINE

When a nation's leader is under spiritual siege, will you answer the call to stand in the gap?

Standing in the Gap for The President: 50 Days of Prayer for Leadership, Loyalty, and Lifeline is a bold, Scripture-saturated prayer guide for those who understand that the battles facing our leaders are more than political—they are spiritual. Assassination attempts, betrayal from within, and attacks on character and conscience are not just headlines—they're signs of the times. Inside, you'll find 50 days of strategic intercession divided into three high-impact sections: **Presidential Character & Leadership, Against Disloyal Insiders**, and **Against Assassination Attempts**. The future of a nation can shift through the prayers of the faithful. It's time to stand in the gap.

www.ingramcontent.com/pod-product-compliance
Lightning Source LLC
Chambersburg PA
CBHW062022040426
42447CB00010B/2106